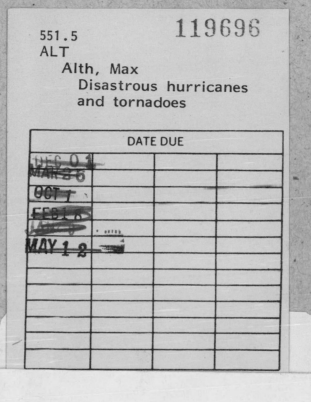

Disastrous Hurricanes and Tornadoes

by Max and Charlotte Alth

Franklin Watts
New York/London/Toronto/Sydney/1981
A First Book

*Frontispiece: this satellite photo,
taken on August 8, 1980, shows
Hurricane Allen in the Gulf of Mexico,
as well as other weather systems.*

Photographs courtesy of
NASA: opp. p. 1, 53;
NOAA: pp. 2, 17, 28, 38, 39 (both), 55, 59;
New York Public Library Picture Collection: p. 5;
United Press International: pp. 25, 27, 36, 61.

Cover photograph courtesy of
Frederick Lewis/Harold Lambert

Library of Congress Cataloging in Publication Data

Alth, Max, 1917–
Disastrous hurricanes and tornadoes.

(A First book)
Includes index.
Summary: Discusses types of wind, how their
force is measured, the characteristics of hurricanes and tornadoes, some devastating storms,
weather proverbs, and safety precautions to take
during hurricanes and tornadoes.
1. Tornadoes—Juvenile literature. 2. Hurricanes—Juvenile literature. [1. Tornadoes.
2. Hurricanes] I. Alth, Charlotte. II. Title.
QC955.A47   551.5′52   81-7544
ISBN 0-531-04327-4   AACR2

Contents

Dedicated to

Misch
Michael
Syme
Darcy
Arabella
Mendel

And everyone else
who runs and
hides at the
sound of thunder.

Disastrous Hurricanes and Tornadoes

Foreword

Mark Twain, author of *The Adventures of Tom Sawyer* and other famous stories, once said, "Everybody talks about the weather, but no one ever does anything about it." Naturally. There is very little we can do about changing the weather.

Weather is brought to us on the wings of the wind. The wind comes and goes as it pleases. We cannot stop the wind, and we cannot change its direction. The wind, of course, is the air around us in motion. During our entire lifetime, from our first breath to our last, we are surrounded by a sea of air. When we swim under water we hold a quantity of air in our lungs. Without air we cannot live for more than five minutes.

When the air around us is almost motionless, we say the day is *calm*. When the air moves slowly, we call it a *light breeze*. When it moves faster, we call it a *fresh breeze,* and when it moves faster still, we call it a *high wind*. When the speed of the wind is more than 74 miles (120 km) per hour, we have what is classified as a *hurricane*.

*Hurricane winds blow down trees
and bring the seas up on shore.*

Scientists disagree on top hurricane wind speeds. Some estimate that the wind in a hurricane never travels much faster than 250 miles (400 km) per hour. Others say hurricane wind speeds can reach 600 miles (960 km) per hour. In any case, no one knows for certain. High winds or flying debris have always destroyed the instruments used to measure hurricane wind speeds.

1

Ancient Winds

In ancient Babylonia, four thousand years ago, it was generally believed that the world was one huge box. The surface of the earth on which the people stood formed the floor or bottom of the box. A huge ocean completely surrounded the earth, and this ocean, in turn, was surrounded by tall mountains that supported the sky.

To the ancient Egyptians, the world was a very different place. Egypt is mainly a flat plateau. When an Egyptian looks across the sands toward the horizon, he or she appears to be looking upward. The ancient Egyptians, therefore, believed the bottom of their world to be dished. From what they could see, Egypt obviously lay in the middle of a huge, shallow depression.

The Babylonians believed that everything in their world—the sky, the earth, the sun, moon, and planets, even the rivers and lakes—was controlled by an individual god. And the position of the sun, they believed, controlled the force and direction of the winds that blew across their land.

A depiction of the Aztec god of the winds

The early Greeks believed that each wind was controlled by an individual god. That is, there was a god who ruled the wind that blew from the north, another who had charge of the wind that blew from the south, and so on. Later Greeks decided that the task could be done by just one god. They called him Aeolus.

Aeolus kept the wind in a huge cave with twelve holes. Each hole was covered by a stone. When he wanted the wind to blow from a particular direction, Aeolus would roll away the stone covering one of the holes. To produce a storm, he would uncover all of the openings at one time.

Aristotle (384–322 B.C.), a Greek and the leading scientist of his day, stated that all winds were emanations of the earth produced by the sun. When the sun was weak, as in winter, the emanations were cold and damp, and rain would fall. When the sun was strong, the wind would blow hot and dry.

Aristotle put his ideas on wind and weather into a book he called *Meteorologica*. During the 1,900 years that followed, until the sixteenth century, most people accepted these ideas as pure fact. Even our name for the science of weather, *meteorology*, comes from the title of Aristotle's book.

In ancient days there were many theories on the nature of matter. One suggested that the universe was made of just one thing, air. Everything a person saw, touched, or smelled was a kind of air.

Another theory held that there were four elements making up the universe: fire, water, earth, and air. The Greek mathematician and philosopher Pythagoras (582–507 B.C.) argued for this theory.

We now know that there are at least 104 natural elements making up our world and that air is a combination of elements, including gases such as oxygen and nitrogen.

Air was a puzzle for thousands of years. Did it have weight? The great Italian astronomer, Galileo Galilei (1564–1642), thought it did. He also thought, as did the ancients, that "nature abhors [hates] a vacuum." But he was puzzled by the fact that a suction pump, at sea level, could only raise a column of water to a height of 34 feet (10.4 m).

When you sip soda through a straw, you are behaving like a suction pump. A mechanical pump works the same way as a human pump. In a mechanical pump, though, there is a large pipe instead of a straw, and, in place of your contracting cheeks, there is a piston within the pipe. When the piston is pulled upward, water follows to fill the vacuum left by the air pulled out.

Galileo speculated that if nature did indeed abhor a vacuum, the column of water in the pump should keep rising indefinitely. He surmised, incorrectly, that a column of water longer than 34 feet (10.4 m) must simply break under its own weight.

Galileo is generally credited with having invented a water thermometer, a crude device for measuring air temperature. It was this work, plus his experiments with the suction pump, that laid the groundwork for a young Italian disciple of Galileo's, Evangelista Torricelli (1608–1647), to invent an instrument that could detect and even measure air pressure, thereby proving that air has weight (since a substance that has no weight cannot exert pressure). Today we call Torricelli's invention a *mercury barometer* and use it to forecast the weather. Weather reports almost always include *barometric pressure readings* and recent changes in pressure, if there are any, since so many of our weather patterns result from changes in air pressure.

Torricelli's instrument consisted of a glass tube filled with mercury, sealed at one end and turned upside down. Its open end was in a dish of mercury.

As the temperature of the air rose, the mercury expanded, and its height increased inside the glass tube. As the temperature dropped, the column of mercury dropped. However, there were also days when the temperature of the air did not change but the height of the mercury did. Why?

Torricelli said that the column of mercury rose and fell with changes in the weight of the air around it, changes in the barometric pressure. Other scientists, to test Torricelli's claim, took the instrument to the top of a mountain, where the air is thinner, and found that the pressure did indeed decrease as one ascended.

Air weighs about 1/800th as much as water. At sea level, the total weight of the air over our heads amounts to 14.7 pounds per square inch (1.0 kg/sq cm). When a suction pump's piston moves up, it is the weight of the air pushing against the water that causes the water to go up the pipe. In a mercury barometer, the weight of the air pushing against the mercury is exactly equal to the weight of the column of mercury.

Modern barometers are calibrated in inches. Normally, a barometer at sea level will read 29.9 inches (76 cm), which means that the pressure of the air at that point and at that moment is exactly equal to the weight of a column of mercury of the same height. If the same barometer, still at sea level, shows a higher or lower reading, it means that the pressure of the air at that point has increased or decreased—which it will with changes in the weather.

Suppose that instead of remaining at the seashore, we carry our barometer up the side of a mountain. As we ascend, we notice that the reading drops. The higher we go, the lower the barometer reads. This is because the amount of air over our heads decreases as we go up. If we could somehow take our barometer to 100,000 feet (30,000 m), it would indicate almost zero pressure, since 99 percent of the earth's atmosphere would be below us. A few miles further out from earth, we leave the last few molecules of air behind us and enter the almost perfect vacuum of outer space.

It is the movement of this roughly 19-mile (30-km)-high ocean of air covering our earth that gives us our breezes and storms and carries water from the oceans and lakes to provide us with life-sustaining rain.

2

The Wind Has a Thousand Names

Winds differ. They differ in speed, direction, temperature, duration, and content. They blow across all lands and many different types of people. In some instances, the same wind may have several names simply because the people it touches have different languages. More often, the winds are called by different names because they *are* different. They come and go at different times of the year or blow from different directions. Some winds are very welcome in that they bring warmth and needed rain. Others are hated and feared because they bring death and destruction. Some are friends because you can depend on them to drive your sailboat in the direction you wish to go. Others are enemies that will fill your eyes with sand or cover your fields with tons of dust.

Wind Scale

Weather vanes were invented and in use very early in history. Even without them, though, people had little trouble identifying wind direction, and they described the winds by the direction from which they came. North winds blew out of the north. An east wind blew from the east. We still name our winds the same way. Wind speed is much more of a problem.

Up until 1755, when Samuel Johnson completed the first English dictionary, people writing in English could spell words any way they wished, and they often did.

Up until 1805, sailors and navigators could describe wind speeds any way *they* wished, and *they* usually did. A fair wind to one person might be a strong wind to another. To eliminate this confusion, in 1805 Sir Francis Beaufort, an admiral in the British navy, devised his now-famous Beaufort scale. Beaufort gave the wind numbers, names, and specific ranges of wind speed. For example, a wind moving at a speed of 4 to 7 miles (6.4 to 11.2 km) per hour had a rating of 2 on the Beaufort scale and was called a light breeze. A light breeze can be felt on one's face; it will cause leaves to rustle and weather vanes to turn. He gave hurricanes a rating of 12 or more and said that they caused great damage and widespread destruction.

Beaufort's scale was fine, but its usefulness was limited. The fault was not his. The instruments of his day were not very accurate or precise. The first really dependable *anemometers,* or wind-speed measuring instruments, were not constructed until 1850 or so.

Winds may be classified by type as well as by speed. There are three major types of winds: local, regional, and global.

Local Winds

Local winds are *convection winds,* meaning that the wind is caused by cold air moving in to replace warmer air that has

THE BEAUFORT
SCALE
OF WIND FORCE

Beaufort Number	Terms Used by Weather Bureau	Wind Effects Observed on Land	Miles Per Hour	Knots
0	*Calm*	Smoke rises vertically	Less than 1	Less than 1
1	*Light air*	Direction of wind shown by smoke drift but not by wind vanes	1–3	1–3
2	*Light breeze*	Wind felt on face, leaves rustle, ordinary vane moved by wind	4–7	4–6
3	*Gentle breeze*	Leaves and small twigs in constant motion; wind extends light flag	8–12	7–10
4	*Moderate breeze*	Raises dust, loose paper; small branches are moved	13–18	11–16
5	*Fresh breeze*	Small trees begin to sway; wavelets form on inland waters	19–24	17–21

6	*Strong breeze*	Large branches in motion; whistling heard in telegraph wires; umbrellas used with difficulty	25–31	22–27
7	*High wind (near gale)*	Whole trees in motion; walking against wind difficult	32–38	28–33
8	*Gale*	Twigs break off trees; wind generally impedes pedestrian traffic	39–46	34–40
9	*Strong gale*	Slight structural damage occurs (chimney pots, slates removed); large branches broken	47–54	41–47
10	*Whole gale*	Seldom experienced inland; trees uprooted; considerable structural damage occurs	55–63	48–55
11	*Storm*	Very rarely experienced; accompanied by widespread damage	64–73	56–63
12 or more	*Hurricane*	Very rarely experienced; accompanied by widespread and extreme damage	74 or more	64 or more

risen. Convection winds blow from areas of high barometric pressure to areas where the barometric pressure is low. *Sea breezes, land breezes, mountain winds,* and *valley winds* are all simple convection winds.

Sea breezes. These are breezes that blow directly in from the sea and across the land every day. In temperate zones, sea breezes will reach a top speed of only 12 miles (19 km) per hour and will travel no more than 10 miles (16 km) inland. In the tropics, sea breezes may reach speeds of 24 miles (38 km) per hour and travel inland as much as 100 miles (160 km).

Sea breezes are caused by daytime temperature differences between the sea and the adjoining land. During the day, the air over the ground heats up much more quickly than the air over the sea. Since warm air tends to rise, the air over the land begins to rise, and the cooler air over the sea flows inland to replace it.

Sea breezes usually start moving by mid-morning, reach their top speed in the middle of the afternoon, when the sea is at its warmest, and come to a complete stop by eight or nine o'clock in the evening.

Land breezes. These, too, are produced by temperature differences, but land breezes move in the exact opposite direction of sea breezes. When the sun has set, the air over the land cools much more rapidly than the air over the sea. The air over the sea stays warmer than the air over the land, and it begins to rise. As it does so, the cooler air from above the land flows seaward to replace it and to equalize the pressure differences.

Sea/land breezes are particularly welcome in warm countries. There, they are often given poetic names.

Mountain winds. Mountains also cause convection winds. These winds are sometimes called *thermal slope winds*. They are produced by the temperature differences between the sides of a mountain and the adjoining valley floor. The rising sun's rays strike the sides of the mountain long before they reach the valley floor. In addition, rocky mountainsides heat up much more rapidly than the grass- or tree-covered valley. As a result, the air over the mountains is warmer than the air over the valley, and during the day the air flows up the sides of the mountain. At night, the rocky mountainsides cool more rapidly than the valley, and the air flows down the mountainsides.

Valley winds. When the valley between two or more mountains is long and deep, for example, as in the Alps or in the High Sierras, the mountain wind not only blows up the sides of the mountain during the day, it also flows along the whole length of the valley from its widest to its narrowest end. Very often this valley wind is hot and dusty. In some valleys, it has blown steadily for so many years that it has bent trees and removed many of their leaves. At night, the valley wind blows gently in the opposite direction.

Regional Winds

Temperature differences also produce regional winds. The *chinook* is an example of a regional wind. Regional winds differ from sea/land winds mainly in that they travel much farther. The chinook is a warm, snow-melting wind that appears each spring. It flows down the eastern slopes of the Rocky Mountains and has been welcomed for thousands of years by the Chinook Indians who inhabit that region. Another warming, downslope seasonal wind is the famed *foehn* of the Alps, and still another is the *Santa Ana* of southern California.

Not all regional winds bring warmth or are welcomed. The fierce *mistral* that rushes down the Rhone Valley of France is neither warm nor loved. Strabo (63 B.C.–A.D. 24), a Greek geographer, wrote of it some two thousand years ago. "A terrible, icy wind that moves rocks, hurls men from their chariots, crushes their limbs, strips them of their clothing and weapons," was how he described the mistral. This regional, northerly wind starts in the high central plateau of France and blows southward to the Mediterranean. When the mistral squeezes through the narrow Rhone River Valley it speeds up, hurls rocks through windows, and damages buildings. Once it pushed a string of railroad cars 25 miles (40 km) before the cars could be stopped.

The *bora* is another icy regional wind. It originates in Russia and roars downhill toward the coast of the Adriatic Sea (an arm of the Mediterranean), sometimes at speeds of up to 100 miles (160 km) per hour. The name is believed to have come from Boreas, the Greek god of the north wind.

The mistral and the bora are called *fall winds* by some meteorologists because they literally "fall" downhill as a result of the heavy weight of the cold air.

Monsoons. Monsoons are regional winds that are also considered global winds by many scientists because they cover so much of our globe.

The word *monsoon* is Arabic and means "season." It is estimated that half of the world's population depends on food grown with the aid of water brought from distant seas by seasonal monsoon winds and rains. The same monsoons have also caused the death of countless millions by bringing too much water at once to some lands.

The most important monsoon is the South Asian monsoon that blows across India and Pakistan. This is followed in size by the East Asian monsoon that travels across China and Japan. Smaller monsoons blow over northern Australia, the Gulf of

*Not all winds are welcome. The tree that
struck this Bethesda, Maryland, home
in 1980 was toppled by strong winds.*

Guinea in western Africa, some parts of eastern Africa, and the Gulf of Mexico.

The South Asian monsoon results from seasonal temperature differences between the landmass of central Asia and the Indian Ocean and Arabian Sea. During the winter, the land is colder than the ocean and sea, and the atmospheric pressure over central Asia is higher than the pressure over the water. The wind, therefore, blows southwest from Asia down across India. The winter monsoon wind is dry and cool.

With the coming of summer, the Asian landmass warms up. The air above it warms up, and the barometric pressure rises. The vast ocean and sea do not warm up as quickly. The air over the water remains cool, with a pressure higher than that of the air over central Asia. The cool, comparatively high-pressure air moves northeast to replace the air rising over central Asia. The monsoon is really a gigantic sea/land breeze that takes place once a year instead of once a day.

The summer monsoon that brings the eagerly awaited rain to India usually reaches the coast at the beginning of June. Usually, but not always. In 1972, the monsoon rains were three weeks late, and India lost nearly one-third of its food crop. In the year that followed, the rains were on time, and crop production was normal. One year later, in 1974, Bangladesh, which is physically but no longer politically a part of India, was struck by very heavy early rains that caused many deaths and tremendous damage. Elsewhere in India that year, the rains were again late.

The quantity of water a monsoon can carry is both unbelievable and unpredictable. In some years, the rainfall can be twice that of other years. Some parts of the Indian subcontinent, particularly along the southwestern coast and in the area of the Ganges River delta, the annual rainfall is 100 inches (254 cm). At Cherrapunji, which is near the border of Bangladesh, the summer monsoon brings an average of 436 inches (1,107 cm) of rain each year. The average annual rainfall in the United States is only 30 inches (76 cm) and is spread over most of the year.

Global Winds

Global winds are produced by the temperature differences between the poles and the equator. Since these differences do not change very much with changes in the seasons, global winds blow constantly and always in the same direction. Since the distance from the equator to either pole is roughly one-fourth the distance around the earth, global winds form the major wind systems of our earth.

If the earth did not spin, but remained stationary, hot air rising above the equator would divide into two streams. One would flow northward toward one pole. The other would flow southward toward the other pole. At the poles the air would become chilled, sink down toward the earth, and flow back toward the equator.

However, the earth does spin, or rotate, and its spinning affects the global winds blowing from the equator to the poles in two ways. One way is friction. The earth rotates from west to east, and in so doing tends to drag the air along with it. This creates friction.

The second way is the Coriolis effect, named after the nineteenth-century French mathematician, Gaspard Gustave de Coriolis, who first recognized it. This effect, which becomes stronger as you approach the poles, acts to bend or deflect winds.

North-seeking winds above the equator are deflected toward the west, and south-seeking winds below the equator are deflected toward the east.

Together, these two factors churn the air into huge masses of circling wind. In the northern hemisphere, these circling air masses always travel counterclockwise. Below the equator, they always travel in the opposite direction.

The doldrums. Where the air descends and rises, there is little horizontal air movement, little wind. Rising air is of no help to a sailor. Therefore, the two broad bands of almost windless air near the equator, known as the *doldrums,* were hated and feared by sailors. It was here that the sea turned to glass, and ships could lie becalmed for weeks, sometimes soaked by a torrential downpour. Also called the *equatorial calms,* the heated air in these 50- to 100-mile (80- to 160-km)-wide bands of sea rises almost vertically and divides roughly in half. One-half of the rising air heads north toward the north pole. The other half moves south toward the south pole. Both masses of air grow cool more or less above the latitudes of 30°North and 30°South. There, the air descends, grows warm again, rises, and resumes its journey to the pole.

North of the doldrums is another calm area best known as the "horse latitudes." Spanish ships sailing to the New World often found themselves becalmed in these waters. It is said that as their supply of drinking water dwindled, they were forced to stop watering their horses. The horses died of thirst and were thrown overboard.

The trade winds. If we start at the equator and travel directly north 50 or so miles (80 km), we come to the edge of that huge mass of circling air mentioned above. Here we find a dependable, steady wind that always blows from the northeast. This is the wind that brought Columbus from Europe to the New World—and is said to have frightened his crew. How, they wondered, would they ever work their way back against a wind that blew so steadily in one direction?

The wind they were referring to is called a *trade wind,* after the old word used for path or track. The trade wind got its name because it is so steady that it appears to be following a track.

If we were to follow Columbus to the West Indies and then head north along the Atlantic coast and west after we were above the horse latitudes, we could pick up the *westerlies.* This is the northern portion of that huge mass of circling air, and it, too, is a trade wind. But it is most often called the mid-latitude westerlies or just the westerlies. With this wind at our backs and a stout clipper ship beneath our feet, we could sail from New York to London in twelve or thirteen days.

Jet streams. Jet streams are huge rivers of air found within our atmosphere in the temperate zones at altitudes of 10,000 to 40,000 feet (3,000 to 12,000 m). They race around the earth from west to east like huge snakes, curving now toward the equator and now back toward the poles. Each jet may be thousands of miles long, hundreds of miles wide, and several thousand feet thick. They come and go as they wish, with no predictable pattern. Their speeds will vary from 75 to 350 miles (120 to 560 km) per hour. Strangely, the speed of the air inside the jet stream may be 100 miles (160 km) per hour higher than the speed of the air at the edges.

Generally, there are three jet streams in each half of the globe in the winter and two in the summer. None of them remain fixed in their paths. They will shift, curve in one direction, then curve in another. Sometimes a jet will split into two jets only to re-form as one many miles further along.

Since the wind is invisible, we did not know that jet streams existed until World War II. This was when pilots of high-flying planes found themselves flying over the ground a lot faster or slower than their instruments indicated. Planes flying in the same direction as a jet stream picked up the additional speed of the stream. Planes bucking a jet stream arrived hours later than they expected.

Today, our high-flying aircraft seek these jet streams. When your captain says, "We have a tail wind," you will know that your plane is being pushed along by a jet stream.

While it is true that you cannot see jet streams, they often make their presence visible by forming featherlike clouds called *cirrus streamers*. Usually you will see these clouds about 4 to 8 miles (6.4 to 12.8 km) up in the sky on the south side of a jet stream. Below the equator, the cirrus clouds form on the north side of a jet stream.

Hurricanes

Along with tales of a wondrous new land and a few natives to prove his discovery, Columbus also brought back to Spain some bad news—stories about terrible storms the natives of the New World called *hurakans*. Hurricanes were new to Europeans because they do not occur in Europe. Few mariners were familiar with similar storms called tropical cyclones in the Indian Ocean and typhoons in the western Pacific. Australia, where hurricanes are called willy-willies, was yet to be discovered.

All of these windstorms, including hurricanes, typhoons, cyclones, tornadoes, and waterspouts, are the same in that they all rotate around a low-pressure center called an *eye*. In the northern hemisphere, these cyclonic winds always rotate counter-clockwise. In the southern hemisphere, they always rotate clockwise.

Cyclonic winds can be the terror of human existence. Nothing else on earth duplicates their awesome power and size. A hurricane may cover an area hundreds of miles across. The wind circling about its low-pressure center may reach speeds of from 74 to several hundred miles (119 to 320 km) per hour or more. Some scientists estimate that a large hurricane can expend as much energy as one hydrogen bomb exploding every second. Generally, hurricanes last eight to ten days.

Within the eye of the hurricane, the air is balmy. The sky overhead may be clear and blue. The eye may be 10 to 50 miles (16 to 80 km) across. The eye and the terrible winds that circle it may pause for an hour or even half a day. Then they will move on, at speeds of up to 60 miles (96 km) per hour.

Above the equator, hurricanes usually move westward first, then curve northward, and then to the northeast in a giant swing. But this is not always the case. Their exact path is unpredictable. Hurricanes have been known to zigzag, stand still, and even go backward. That is another reason why they are so dangerous.

Navy meteorologists are supposedly among the best. Yet during World War II, Admiral William Halsey of the United States led his Third Fleet into the teeth of a Pacific typhoon, not once but twice.

Cyclonic winds are born at sea, over warm water. Since the sea in the northern hemisphere is warmest in September, most hurricanes originate during this month. But hurricanes have also appeared over the North Atlantic in May and December.

On an average, some ten hurricanes are formed in the North

Atlantic every year. About six of these develop dangerous wind speeds. Usually less than two reach American shores. But there was one year when five terrible hurricanes struck the United States.

The fierce winds of cyclonic storms are not the only cause of death and destruction. Cyclonic storms can dump 12 inches (30 cm) of rain in a few hours. Pouring down a hillside, heavy rainfall can wash away homes and drown animals and humans. The storm's powerful winds push the seas up on shore. These wind-driven waves can reach heights of 40 feet (12 m) or more. They will smash buildings, drive boats far inland, and drown all creatures in their path.

Strangely enough, there are no hurricanes in the South Atlantic Ocean. One reason given is that the waters of the South Atlantic are much cooler than those north of the equator.

Tornadoes

Tornadoes are also cyclonic winds. They rotate at very high speeds around a low-pressure center but are smaller than hurricanes and last a far shorter time. Still, they are more intense than hurricanes and can be just as devastating.

Tornadoes range in size from as little as 100 feet (30 m) across to as much as 1.5 miles (2.4 km) wide. The smallest tornadoes, called minis, have winds speeds of under 100 miles (160 km) per hour. They last no longer than a few minutes. During this time they may travel half a mile (.8 km). The largest tornadoes, called maxis, may be as much as 1.5 miles (2.4 km) across. Maxis may travel 200 miles (320 km) or more, last up to three hours, and have winds speeds of more than 250 miles (400 km) per hour.

Tornadoes are unpredictable and deadly. What they do not smash, drown, explode, or electrocute (by lightning), they

*The funnel of a 1978 tornado snakes
across the sky near Braman, Oklahoma.
Tornadoes are unpredictable and deadly.*

carry away. Once a tornado in Minnesota carried an 83-ton (75-m.t.) railroad coach and 117 passengers 80 feet (24 m) through the air. In Mississippi a tornado once blew a home freezer more than a mile (1.6 km) through the air. People and animals, too, have been hurled through the air. Few survived to tell the tale. At the same time, the devilish wind fills the air with everything that isn't nailed down—chairs, bricks, boards. Everything flies with bullet speed. Many people have survived the wind only to be killed by flying objects.

But the wind that chops buildings neatly in half and picks up objects and smashes them to bits is not all of the calamity. Tornadoes are almost always accompanied by heavy rain, lightning, and hail. Some of the hailstones may be 6 inches (15 cm) or more in diameter.

The eye of a tornado is a partial vacuum. When it passes over a building, it may cause the building to explode, due to unequal air pressures. Fortunately, this does not happen too often. The wind usually rips the building's roof off and knocks its walls down before any explosion can take place.

Passing over water, a tornado creates a *waterspout*. This is a spinning column of water perhaps a mile (1.6 km) high. The column is topped by a giant black cloud that darkens the area and strikes fear into all that see it. Fortunately, waterspouts are comparatively rare, and they do not have the power of tornadoes. However, they have been known to lift small boats into the air and drop them some distance away. Rains of frogs and fishes are believed to be the work of waterspouts.

Tornadoes are not limited to the United States. However, most of the world's tornadoes do strike the U.S. Gulf Coast and central plains. In 1974, for example, the United States was hit by 1,102 tornadoes.

Most tornadoes occur in May. The fewest occur in Decem-

When a tornado passes over a building, it may cause the building to explode. Usually, though, the wind rips the building's roof off before this can happen. Note, for example, how an Omaha tornado in 1975 ripped off the roofs of these buildings.

Two waterspouts near the Bahama Islands

ber. During the so-called "Super Outbreak" of April 3–4 in 1974, 148 tornadoes struck eleven states and Canada. Three hundred and fifty persons died. Damage amounted to more than $600 million.

Most tornadoes are minis. But some are maxis. On March 18, 1925, one maxi traveled 219 miles (350 km) in 195 minutes. It killed 689 people.

The chance of a tornado hitting any particular location is small. But in 1879, Austin, Texas, experienced two tornadoes in rapid succession. Codell, Kansas, was struck three times; once in 1916, once in 1917, and once again in 1918. Each time the tornado struck on May 20.

3

Winds and People

Favorable Winds

The winds, with the help of our oceans and seas, make our weather. Every year the sun evaporates some 95,000 cubic miles (110,000 cu km) of water. We see this water in the form of clouds overhead. If there were no winds, the water—rain—would fall straight down and back into the ocean. No rain would fall on land, and all earth would be a desert.

Winds bring warm, moist air from the tropics to the polar areas of our world. Winds bring cool air from the poles back down to the tropics. Currents in the ocean, caused by wind, help circulate the waters of our world so that the tropic waters are cooler than they might otherwise be and the polar waters are warmer, all of which helps to reduce the temperature differences between the polar regions and the tropics.

Winds wear mountains down, turning them slowly into soil. Winds spread plant seeds and blow loess (fine soil) deposited by rivers back up onto the plains, making the plains more fertile. The winds drive our windmills and sailing ships. Now that fossil fuels are growing scarce, we can expect to see many more windmills and sailing ships in the future.

Winds Interfere

The ancient Greeks often saw winds change their lives. It is no wonder that they believed that each wind was the work of a god.

In the year 480 B.C., Xerxes, the emperor of Persia, sent his 1,200-ship fleet into the Straits of Salamis to destroy the much smaller fleet of the Greek allies. The ships of the Persian fleet were taller than those of the Greeks, and they depended mainly on wind and sail for their movement. The Greeks drove their ships with man-powered oars.

A strong sea breeze sprang up. The Persians could not control their ships, and they ran into each other. Unable to move, the Persian ships were rammed and sunk by the Greeks, who were unaffected by the wind. Xerxes was defeated.

In 1260, Kublai Khan, a grandson of Genghis Khan, ruled the world from what is now Poland in the west to the eastern shores of China. But he was not satisfied. He longed to add Japan to his domains. Being a horseman and not a sailor, Kublai Khan had the king of Korea build a fleet for him. In 1272, the fleet sailed across the Yellow Sea and landed safely. A storm arose. To save their ships, the men went back on board. The storm sank 200 of the 600 vessels and drowned 13,000 of the 40,000 men. The survivors returned to China.

However, Kublai Khan did not give up. In 1281, he sent two fleets with an estimated 150,000 men to attack Japan. Once again they managed to land safely. But the Japanese fought and held them near the shore for six weeks. Then a typhoon struck. Two-thirds of the Mongols died. This time, Kublai Khan did give up.

By some chance or freak of nature, Columbus did not encounter a hurricane in the New World on his first voyage, though he lingered all through the summer, fall, and winter of 1492–93. When he returned to Spain in 1493, he reported, "In all the Indies I have always found the weather like May."

Nor did Columbus personally encounter a hurricane on his second voyage, in 1494. Two of his ships were sunk or driven ashore, but he himself was aboard another ship far away at the time.

In 1502, fortune seekers who followed Columbus to the New World filled the holds of their ships with gold. Despite warnings, a flotilla of twenty vessels set out in the teeth of a hurricane. Nineteen sank to the bottom of the sea off the coast of Puerto Rico.

When Columbus returned to Spain in 1504 after his final voyage, he wrote, in part: "My eyes never beheld seas so high. . . . The wind prevented us from running behind any headland for shelter. . . . We were forced to keep out in this bloody ocean, seething like a pot on a hot fire. The people were so worn out they longed for death to end their dreadful suffering."

Suppose Columbus had met a hurricane head on during his first voyage. How long do you think the discovery of the New World would have been delayed?

In the year 1588, King Philip II of Spain sent his Armada up the English Channel, intending to drive the much smaller English fleet out of the water and invade England. But the English stayed clear and fired at the oncoming Spaniards with their long-range, light guns. In turn, the Spaniards fired their heavy guns at the British. Most of the Spanish shot fell short. Little damage was done to either side.

The Armada anchored off Calais, France. The English sent burning ships downwind into the Spanish fleet. No fires were started amongst the Spanish ships, but the Spanish captains panicked and cut their anchors to get clear. Suddenly a northwest wind blew them toward the shore and certain destruction! Moments later the wind turned around. They were saved.

They were out of ammunition, however. The invasion was now impossible. They decided to sail north, up the English Channel to the North Sea and then around Scotland. From there they would head south for Spain. Back home they would rearm and refit and return the following year.

The wind, however, played them false. Rounding Scotland, the heavy, cumbersome ships were driven ashore. Fifty vessels and 9,000 men never made it back to Spain. Philip gave up his plans to conquer England.

A hurricane stopped the Spaniards from colonizing Florida. In June 1559, some 1,500 Spanish soldiers and settlers set sail for what is now Pensacola, Florida. They reached land without any major trouble and began to disembark when a hurricane struck. Most of their ships were sunk. Hundreds of people were drowned. King Philip II of Spain decided that perhaps Florida wasn't the best place to build his colonies.

Killer Winds:
Cyclones and Hurricanes

It was October 7, 1737, in Bengal, India. A cyclone driving up the Bay of Bengal produced sea waves 40 feet (12 m) high. The waves washed over the Hooghly River delta, killing some 300,000 people and sinking 20,000 small boats. On October 5, 1864, in Calcutta, India, another cyclone drove the sea up over the Hooghly River basin. Much of the city of Calcutta was destroyed and an estimated 70,000 people were drowned. In 1876, a third cyclone that began in the Bay of Bengal struck India. This time storm tides rose 20 feet (6 m) above normal. The offshore islands near Chittagong were engulfed. At least 100,000 people were immediately drowned. An additional 100,000 died from starvation resulting from the loss of their crops.

On October 10, 1780, a storm began in the Caribbean Islands. Called the Great Hurricane because it was the most deadly in the history of the area, it killed an estimated 30,000 people. First the storm struck Barbados. Then it destroyed the British fleet that was anchored on the "safe" side of Saint Lucia. Continuing, the storm crossed the island of Martinique and sank a forty-ship convoy.

In 1881, at Haiphong in Vietnam, driven by a mighty typhoon, the sea rose and flooded the seaport at the mouth of the Red River on the Gulf of Tonkin. Some 300,000 persons were either drowned immediately or died from the starvation and disease that followed the destruction of the port and its facilities.

In September 1900, a hurricane swept west across Puerto Rico, Haiti, and Cuba and entered the Gulf of Mexico. The Weather Bureau in Washington had no observers in the Gulf of Mexico. It would be five more years before ships would begin to send weather reports directly to the Bureau. The Bureau calculated from the information available that the storm would turn north and pass well to the east of the city of Galveston, Texas. Galveston did not prepare. The hurricane paid no attention to the forecast. It hit the city on the nose on the morning of September 7. Galveston is on an island that is only 8 feet (2.4 m) above high tide. The storm pushed the sea ahead of itself. Waves more than 15 feet (4.5 m) high swept over the island. Few buildings remained standing. The following morning, would-be rescuers found the bodies of 6,000 people who had drowned. The bodies of another 2,000 were never recovered. Writing about the tragedy sixty-seven years later, one survivor,

Harry J. Maxon, could still recall people screaming for help that terrible night.

In September 1938, a hurricane originated some 400 miles (640 km) west of Africa. Like a typical hurricane, it moved slowly west at a speed of about 20 miles (32 km) per hour. When it was close enough to Florida to frighten everyone, it paused. Then it began to move directly north. Meteorologists misread the signs. The news media and inhabitants north of the hurricane did not take it seriously. None of them remembered the last tropical storm to hit Long Island and the New England coast some seventy years earlier. Instead of a hurricane warning, a gale warning was broadcast. The hurricane picked up speed. It began to move north at 60 miles (96 km) per hour, driving a huge sea wave 100 miles (160 km) before it.

Frightened by the suddenly darkening skies, the few people on the beaches of southern Long Island took shelter behind the sand dunes. The surging sea struck an hour before the wind. Water swept up the beach and over the dunes, drowning many. Beach houses were smashed, and boats were driven ashore. The wind smashed into the land and crossed the island so fast that the storm was later given the nickname, "Long Island Express."

Then the sky cleared. People came out of their shelters, stunned but grateful to be alive. But the storm was only teasing them. The eye of the hurricane was 40 miles (64 km) across. It passed in thirty minutes. Then the reverse side of the storm hit. Once again, most people were caught unprepared. More death and destruction followed.

The storm continued north. The wind and rain caused the Connecticut River to overflow its banks. Suddenly, the streets of Norwich, Connecticut, were covered with 12 feet (3.6 m) of water. Winds pushed the waters of Narragansett Bay into the streets of Providence, Rhode Island. The time was 5 P.M. People

This excursion steamer was sunk at its pier in Providence, Rhode Island, as a result of the storm that hit Long Island and the New England coast in September 1938.

were just leaving work. Many were drowned in the streets. Others were killed or injured by toppling buildings or flying debris.

Deaths due directly to wind and flooding totaled some 700. Another 1,500 people were injured. A hundred thousand homes were badly damaged or completely destroyed, as were 26,000 automobiles. Three hundred million trees were uprooted and destroyed.

Wind speeds were recorded at 120 miles (193 km) per hour, with gusts estimated at speeds of 250 miles (400 km) per hour. The force of the sea waves striking Long Island and the coast of New England was so great that earthquake instruments as far away as California responded to the events.

Since 1950, hurricanes have been given names. One called Camille, after a flower, hit the states of Mississippi, Louisiana, Alabama, Virginia, and West Virginia in August 1969. It killed at least 300 persons. Storm tides rose to 24 feet (7.3 m) above sea level. Twenty-seven inches (68 cm) of water fell in eight hours, causing flash floods. Wind gusts up to 175 miles (280 km) per hour were recorded.

On November 13, 1970, a cyclone hit the offshore islands of East Pakistan near the Haringhata River and stretches of the coastline near Chittagong. Since most of this land is only a few feet above sea level, the storm surges washed over everything. The land was cleared of houses, animals, people, and crops. One million head of cattle were drowned, and it is thought that an equal number of people might also have been drowned. On some large islands, entire villages were washed away. On thirteen small islands off Chittagong, not one inhabitant remained alive. Some 800,000 tons (726,000 m.t.) of rice disappeared when more than 1,700 square miles (4,400 sq km) of land were flooded by the angry sea. The indifference with which the Pakistan government treated this disaster helped fuel a re-

—37

Damage from Hurricane Camille. The photograph above is of a home in Biloxi, Mississippi. Note that the boat shown on the right was in the water when the hurricane struck. The photograph opposite (left side) shows all that was left of a thirty-two-unit apartment building in Gulfport, Mississippi. The photograph on the right is of another home in Biloxi, Mississippi.

bellion that led to the eventual establishment of the state of Bangladesh.

Killer Winds: Tornadoes

The most destructive single tornado recorded in American history was one of a group of tornadoes that appeared in Reynolds County, Missouri, on the afternoon of March 18, 1925. It differed from other tornadoes in several ways. First, it had no black funnel so it did not look dangerous. Second, it traveled in a straight line and moved very fast—straighter and faster than any other known tornado before or since.

Called the Tri-State Twister because it hit three states, the tornado headed northeast at a speed of 72 miles (115 km) per hour. Striking the small town of Annapolis, Missouri, it destroyed 90 percent of the buildings there and raced on, jumping the Missouri River and entering the state of Illinois, where it smashed into the town of Gorham and flattened every building in the town. Minutes later it appeared in Murphysboro, where it wrecked nearly 150 blocks of houses, some 40 percent of the town. Moving on at undiminished speed, the storm overturned eleven huge steam engines.

Continuing on the same straight line, the tornado tore into East Frankfort, Illinois, where it destroyed sixty-four homes in less than two minutes. The wind was so fierce it drove a large timber through the side of a steel railroad car. A large grain binder was carried a quarter of a mile (.4 km) through the air. An automobile was carried half as far before it was dropped to the ground in a tangle of twisted metal. Ripping its way through a school building, the twister lifted sixteen pupils from their chairs and deposited them 450 feet (135 m) away. They were unharmed, but when they looked back at their school, not a brick, not a board, was still standing.

—40

The tornado raced on to destroy 90 percent of the village of Parrish, Indiana. At Parrish, the tornado veered slightly to the north after traveling some 200 miles (320 km) in an almost straight line. Minutes later it struck the town of Princeton, Indiana, where it flattened 25 percent of the buildings. From Princeton the tornado traveled on for another few miles, then disappeared.

The tornado had been in existence for only three hours and fifteen minutes. Yet it had traveled 219 miles (352 km), killed 689 persons, injured almost 2,000, and caused more than $16 billion in damages—a record that, fortunately, is still unbeaten.

Years later, when the horror of the event was almost forgotten by most, a man from Griffin, Indiana, described his experience: "I saw the storm coming my way and I ran for the railroad station. As I took hold of the door knob on the station door, the storm just jerked the station out of my hand."

A Waco, Texas, twister that struck on May 11, 1935, hit the town of San Angelo first. But the townspeople there were prepared, and only eleven were killed and sixty-six injured. The people of Waco did not prepare. They had been warned, but no one took the warning seriously. The Indians had a legend that no "Dancing Devil" could ever pass between the hills surrounding the town of Waco. Everybody believed this.

As the dark cloud approached, the air pressure in Waco dropped, causing the people to yawn a little. Moments after the storm hit, the front of a downtown theater exploded into the street. The building's roof fell down. Mailboxes flew through the air; shattered glass was everywhere. Buildings were knocked flat.

The twister stayed in town for only two minutes. But during this time, 2 square miles (5 sq km) were completely destroyed, 114 people were killed, and more than 500 people were injured.

4

Fire, Air, Earth, and Water

Fire

On a hot summer day, the sun is only a little hotter than we can bear. On a cloudy or foggy day, the sun appears to be an almost cold, orange-red ball in the sky. Measured by eye alone, the sun seems no larger than the moon. Yet even the ancients realized that the sun was the source of all power—all energy—on earth.

In ancient times, people believed the sun to be a god. They thought the sun god traveled across the sky during the day. During the night his sister, the moon, took over.

The ancients worshiped the sun, but they did not realize its size or enormous power. The sun is 93 million miles (149 million km) from earth. That is why it appears so small. Actually, the sun has a diameter of about 865,000 miles (1,384,000 km). The diameter of the earth is only 7,926 miles (12,681 km). The sun is a stupendous nuclear power plant that constantly converts huge amounts of hydrogen gas into helium and produces energy at the rate of 70,000 horsepower on every square yard of its vast surface. The sun has been doing this for an estimated 5 billion years. Scientists believe that it can continue to do so for at least another 5 billion more.

Since the sun is so far away and radiates its energy in all directions, the earth receives only a tiny fraction of the sun's total energy. However, this tiny fraction amounts to a steady 23 trillion horsepower constantly striking our earth.

Air

If the sunlight were to strike the earth directly, scientists estimate that daylight temperatures at the equator would go to 180°F (82°C) and that nighttime temperatures in the same spot would drop to −220°F (−140°C). But the sun's light does not strike the earth directly. The earth is protected by a blanket of air. The air that you can hardly feel when you move your hand through it weighs an amazing 5,600 trillion tons (5,080 trillion m.t.). Eighty percent of this total weight is water vapor.

Our blanket of air does several things for us. It protects us from most of the ultraviolet light streaming from the sun. This is the light that causes sunburn. The air also acts as a sort of heat-storage system. And when it moves and becomes wind, it carries heat from warm areas to cold and from cold areas to warm.

Earth

The sun's energy that passes through the air and strikes the earth warms it, and although the earth cools rapidly when the sun goes down, it still retains considerable heat. Daytime heat absorbed by the earth keeps nighttime temperatures from dropping too far. Summertime heat retained by the earth helps raise winter temperatures.

The mountains of the earth act to slow winds down.

Sea

The sea is a great heat reservoir. Most of the surface of our globe is covered by water, 71 percent to be more exact. In all there are 197 million square miles (510 million sq km) of ocean surface. The water forming our seas and oceans is not still. There are many currents within our oceans and seas. These currents bring warm water from tropical areas to cooler areas. One such current is the Gulf Stream, which carries warm water from the Bahamas all the way north, past the British Isles. Without the Gulf Stream, Britain would be colder than Newfoundland.

Together the earth, its air, and its water make our climate endurable in much of the world and even pleasant in many parts of the world.

The Confusion Called Weather

Our planet travels around the sun once a year. The trip is 600 million miles (960 million km) long. Since the earth is tilted $23\frac{1}{2}°$ on its axis, the amount of energy striking each hemisphere varies as the earth goes around the sun. This regular variation, of course, is the cause of our seasons.

Land warms and cools more quickly than water. The daily differences cause the sea/land breezes. With changes in season, the temperature differences between large bodies of water and large landmasses change. These seasonal differences cause regional winds and monsoons.

The equator is warmer than the poles. Hot air rises at the equator, divides, and heads north and south. But the earth rotates, and the Coriolis effect prevents these winds from flowing in a direct path from the equator toward the poles. The surface of the spinning earth is not smooth but supports mountains, which reach up through the atmosphere and interfere with the movement of wind. Our seas are not one temperature but contain warm currents and cold currents. The land does not heat up and cool evenly. Mountainsides, which catch the morning sun, grow warm before the deep valleys.

The sun, the revolution and rotation of the earth, air weight and pressure, daily and seasonal temperature changes, warm and cold currents in our oceans, mountains that block the flow of air all work together to produce our weather.

5

Weather Prophets

Not too long ago, everyone was a kind of weather prophet, especially farmers and fishermen. They had to be. There was no Weather Bureau. There were no worldwide organizations collecting information and broadcasting weather reports. People had to do their own forecasting or consult a local "weather prophet."

Local weather prophets were usually able to forecast the weather as a result of some personal affliction or the affliction of an animal they owned. You may laugh now to read that when grandmother's big toe ached it meant that rain was coming; that when it hurt real bad a storm was on its way; and that when Henry's cat covered its eyes with its paws, one could be certain that it was time to go into the storm cellar. Yet afflictions such as these are still good indicators of changes in barometric pressure.

People with sinus infections—and there are millions—develop headaches when the barometer changes suddenly. Animals, too, can feel this pressure change. They will place their paws over the painful areas. Some will lie in a corner and whine. People with rheumatism or improperly healed bone fractures also feel pain when the weather is about to change suddenly. When the weather has stabilized, the pain usually goes away.

Reliable weather prophets of yesteryear also *did* something others didn't do. They watched the weather, and they remembered. They learned to connect certain cloud shapes with certain kinds of weather. They studied animal behavior in relation to changes in the weather. They memorized the kinds of weather different winds brought at different times of the year.

They knew it wasn't going to rain heavily every summer. A dry summer had to come along just to even things up. A mild winter usually followed a harsh winter.

The Old Farmer's Almanac has been published once a year ever since 1792. The editors of this publication work from records of past weather to forecast the weather for an entire year to come. They make their forecasts the way old-time weather prophets did. They work from the history of the weather and not from daily weather reports, the way modern weather forecasters do. Surprisingly, *The Old Farmer's Almanac* has a comparatively good record of forecasting success.

Weather Proverbs

Here are a number of weather proverbs that have come down to us over the years. They are not always to be relied upon. However, they do contain some truth, or they would not have survived through the years.

Mares' tails and mackerel scales warn lofty ships to trim their sails.

Mares' tails and mackerel scales are traditional names of cirrus and cirrocumulus clouds. These are high, fast-moving clouds that usually indicate a change in the weather.

Rain slow in coming takes long in going. Rain that falls quick, gives a man hardly time to spit.

When rain clouds fill the sky and move slowly in your direction, you can be pretty certain that the clouds cover a vast expanse of land. These rain clouds moving slowly will take a long time to pass overhead. On the other hand, a sudden shower from a cloud that approaches quickly will not last long. The cloud area is small and moving rapidly.

Rainbows in the morning gives shepherds fair warning. Rainbows at night are the shepherds delight.

Rainbows are caused by sunlight striking rain. Most of our weather comes from the west. Therefore, if you are looking west (in the morning), the rain is coming toward you. If you see the rainbow in the evening, you must be looking east. The rain has passed you.

Dark clouds in the west, best stay indoors and rest.

This is another form of the rainbow proverb. Since most of our weather comes from the west, dark clouds in the west are coming toward us. Dark clouds usually mean bad weather.

When ditches and ponds offend one's nose, winds and storms will surely blow.

When air pressure drops, the smelly gases that are dissolved in stagnant pond and ditch water supposedly come more readily to the surface.

When bats and birds hug the ground, wind and hail are sure to pound.

Bats and birds are sensitive to air pressure. When a low-pressure area approaches, they tend to fly lower, where the air pressure is slightly higher. Bees return to their hive when a storm is brewing. They, too, can sense the change in the air pressure, and they are afraid of the rain.

When frogs croak, it's no joke.

The air is often more humid than normal before a storm. This permits frogs to remain out of the water longer and give vent to their croaking for longer periods of time.

The thicker they spin, the stronger the wind.

Spiders, too, sense the low air pressure that comes before a storm. They will make their webs smaller and stronger when they sense bad weather coming.

When the sunset is clear, a cold night is near.

Clouds keep the earth warm. A clear sky lets a lot of heat escape into space.

Some Practical Tips

• A north wind usually means cold weather is coming.

• A south wind usually means warm weather is coming.

• When low clouds move in beneath high clouds, you can expect snow or rain.

• Rain or snow is likely when clouds pile up, one on top of another.

• Skies will clear when dark clouds grow thin and move higher in the skies.

• There is a good chance of frost when fog or dew forms over a pond or lake.

• There is a good chance of rain when leaves turn over. This is usually caused by a south wind leading a cold front.

• Snow will not fall unless the temperature is below freezing and above 20°F (−6.6°C).

• Large snowflakes usually indicate a short snowfall.

• Small snowflakes usually mean the snow will keep falling for a long time.

6

Scientific Forecasting

In the Beginning

For 2,000 years, people interested in knowing the weather before it reached them read the *Book of Signs,* written about 300 B.C. by Theophrastus, a pupil of Aristotle's. In this book, Theophrastus describes two hundred portents (signs) that reveal the weather to come. Some foretell the weather years ahead. Others give only a day's warning. Theophrastus advises his readers to observe the way a centipede crawls, the way sheep behave, and so on. All he lists are weather indicators. Surprisingly, a good percentage of his signs have been found to be generally true.

Over the last few centuries, people have tried to find patterns in the weather. Ships' captains kept records in their log books. A few scientists made weather their main interest. Many of the leaders of the American Revolution were keenly interested in the weather and kept records. George Washington, James Madison, John Quincy Adams, Thomas Jefferson, and, of course, Benjamin Franklin—all kept weather records. According to their records, the temperature in the northeast at 6 A.M., the morning of July 4, 1776, was 68°F (20°C).

Pushed by farmers and Great Lakes steamship companies, a resolution was introduced in Congress in early 1870 and signed by President Ulysses S. Grant on February 9 of that year. The resolution called for the establishment of the U.S. Weather Bureau, to be given an annual budget of $15,000.

Today, in place of army surgeons mailing weather observations to Washington, D.C., the Bureau receives hundreds of reports daily by radio and teletype from weather satellites circling the earth from space, ships at sea, commercial and military aircraft, its own surface observatories, radar stations, and high-flying balloons.

First sent aloft on April 1, 1960, the weather satellites have sensors that can measure temperature and humidity at different distances from the ground and cameras that can take daytime and nighttime pictures. Radioed to ground stations, these pictures show clouds, cloud heights, land and sea surface temperatures, sea ice, snowfields, and storm systems. Some of the satellites are in synchronistic orbit, which means that they travel as fast as the earth turns, so that they appear to be standing still above one spot on earth. Synchronistic orbits are 22,300 miles (35,880 km) above the earth. Other satellites orbit the earth at heights of about 900 miles (1,450 m) once every 115 minutes.

The Start of the Bureau

Dr. James Tilton, physician and surgeon general of the United States Army, is credited with organizing the first American

This September 3, 1975 photograph of Hurricane Katrina,
as it sits off the coast of Baja, California, was taken by
a NASA weather satellite in synchronistic orbit.

weather observation network. On May 2, 1814, he ordered his surgeons to record the weather and note down how it and climate affected diseases. Twenty-four years later, army surgeons in thirteen forts were making daily weather observations. By 1864, there were 143 such weather stations.

But the military was not the only organization collecting weather information during these years. In 1846, the Smithsonian Institution was established in Washington, D.C. By 1849, Joseph Henry, secretary of the Smithsonian, had secured the help of 150 widely scattered volunteer weather reporters. He had also arranged with the telegraph companies to provide free transmission of his observers' weather reports. (It was only several years earlier, on May 24, 1844, that the first telegraph had gone into operation between Baltimore and Washington.) Less than one year later, Henry mounted a weather map and hung it in the hall of the Institution, where it could be seen by the public. It was the first constantly updated map of its kind in the world.

In Cincinnati, Professor Cleveland Abbe, director of the Cincinnati Astronomical Observatory, began issuing a Weather Bulletin. The first weather forecast ever published was printed and distributed on September 22, 1869.

All of the information gathered today is sent to the Bureau's National Meteorological Center in Suitland, Maryland. There, since 1958, incoming meteorological data has been fed into a giant computer. With the help of this computer, the National Weather Service provides thirty-day general forecasts, five-day general forecasts, detailed twenty-four-hour forecasts, reports on weather conditions at over 300 airports, and twelve-hour aviation forecasts that are accurate more than 85 percent of the time. In addition, the Service also issues weather maps, special bulletins, and storm and frost warnings.

*Daily weather forecasts are often
made on the basis of satellite photographs
such as this one taken by NOAA.*

How Accurate is Weather Forecasting?

As we have seen, our weather consists of boiling, churning winds responding to changes in temperature, pressure, and the rotation of the earth. Although scientists have been searching for years, no definite, repeating pattern of weather behavior has ever been found.

However, we do know the general patterns of wind flow, and, by using weather maps, which show readings for wind speed, temperature, barometric pressure, and precipitation, our weather forecasters can make fairly good predictions of our weather. Knowing the wind's speed, temperature, and water or snow content, they can estimate how long it will take to reach their area. Of course, the shorter the time between forecast and event, the more accurate the forecast will be. The National Weather Service, as stated above, is correct about 85 percent of the time with their twelve-hour forecasts.

7

RUN, DON'T WALK

Every year thousands of people die because they have ignored the weather. They go about their lives as if the sun will shine every day. The worst they can imagine is that they will get a little wet or a little cold. They can't imagine drowning in desert country. They can't believe that ocean waves will come way up on shore. The thought of winds that blow trains through the air makes them laugh. They don't watch the weather. They don't heed storm warnings. They don't do what they are told by the authorities.

Watch and Listen

Make it your business to keep an eye on the weather. Take a look at the sky in the morning and again in the evening. Learn what the storm seasons are in your area. Learn where the shelters are in your school and in public buildings in the area.

Listen to the radio or TV stations in your area for weather

reports. All broadcast stations give them. If you want minute-by-minute reports, twenty-four hours a day, listen to the special NOAA weather radio. NOAA stands for *N*ational *O*ceanic and *A*tmospheric *A*dministration. It is part of the U.S. Department of Commerce. NOAA operates the National Weather Service, which does the actual forecasting.

NOAA has more than 300 weather stations. To receive its reports, you need a radio with a weather band or button. As mentioned above, there is a special radio that will pick up all of the three weather channels—162.55 mHz, 162.4 mHz, and 162.475 mHz.

The weather broadcasters often issue "advisories." These are simply warnings to listeners to take certain precautions. For example, when you hear a STORM WATCH advisory, it means there is a good chance that a storm will strike your area in a day or two. On the other hand, STORM WARNING means that a storm is going to strike in twenty-four hours or less. Remember, storms veer and shift and speed up. No one knows for certain just how much time there will be before the storm strikes.

Reading the Signs

Hurricanes are born hundreds or thousands of miles out at sea. They move slowly and are watched from birth by aircraft and weather satellites and tracked on radar.

You can generally recognize an oncoming hurricane. The wind may be gusty or steady, but it will be more or less continuous. The rain may be light or heavy, but it will go on and on. A hurricane can cover hundreds of miles, so the sky will be dark just about everywhere. As the hurricane moves toward you, wind speed will increase.

Scientists working at the National Hurricane Center in Miami, Florida, help predict the paths hurricanes will take.

Sample Hurricane Messages

SAMPLE ADVISORY

NATIONAL HURRICANE CENTER HURRICANE ADVISORY NUMBER 20 LADY NOON EDT SATURDAY AUGUST 28 1971.

THE WEATHER SERVICE ADVISES THAT A HURRICANE EMERGENCY WARNING HAS BEEN ISSUED FOR BOTH SIDES OF THE FLORIDA PENINSULA FROM STUART AND VENICE SOUTHWARD INCLUDING LAKE OKEECHOBEE AND THE KEYS SOUTHWARD AS FAR AS TAVERNIER. A DANGEROUS HURRICANE NOW THREATENS MOST OF SOUTH FLORIDA. SAFETY PRECAUTIONS SHOULD BE RUSHED WITH ALL POSSIBLE URGENCY ON THE SOUTHEAST COAST AND COMPLETED BY NO LATER THAN 6 PM SATURDAY AND SHOULD BE STARTED ON THE WEST COAST SOUTH OF TARPON SPRINGS.

ALL PERSONS IN THE COASTAL AREA FROM MIAMI TO STUART ARE URGED TO EVACUATE IMMEDIATELY BEFORE RISING WATERS CUT OFF ESCAPE. FOR DETAILED INFORMATION ON EVACUATION CONSULT THE LATEST ADVICES FROM LOCAL PUBLIC OFFICIALS. EVACUATION RECOMMENDATIONS FOR THE WEST COAST WILL NOT BE MADE AT THIS TIME BUT THERE WILL BE DANGEROUSLY HIGH STORM TIDES TOMORROW SUNDAY AS FAR NORTH AS VENICE.

MANY INLAND LOW PLACES IN SOUTHERN FLORIDA ARE ALREADY SATURATED OR HAVE STANDING WATER DUE TO THE HEAVY SUMMER RAINS. THE TORRENTIAL RAINFALL EXPECTED FROM THIS HURRICANE WILL ADD AN ADDITIONAL FOOT OR TWO OF WATER IN MANY LOW PLACES.

THERE IS A POSSIBILITY OF A FEW TORNADOES IN SOUTHEAST FLORIDA THIS AFTERNOON ASSOCIATED WITH RAIN SQUALLS WHICH ARE EXPECTED IN ADVANCE OF THE HURRICANE

AT NOON EDT . . . 1600Z . . . THE CENTER OF HURRICANE LADY WAS ESTIMATED ABOUT 225 MILES SOUTHEAST OF MIAMI OR NEAR LATITUDE 24.8 NORTH LONGITUDE 77.0 WEST. HOWEVER AT THAT TIME THE FORWARD EDGE OF THE DANGEROUS WINDS WAS ONLY 80 MILES EAST OF MIAMI. THE STORM IS MOVING TOWARD THE WEST NORTHWEST AT ABOUT 12 MPH. LITTLE CHANGE IN THE SPEED AND DIRECTION OF THE STORM IS EXPECTED DURING THE NEXT 12 HOURS.

MAXIMUM SUSTAINED WINDS ARE ESTIMATED AT 125 MPH BRIEFLY HIGHER IN GUSTS NEAR THE CENTER WITH HURRICANE FORCE WINDS

—60

*Hurricane winds and rains brought
exceptionally high tides to the shores
around this Coast Guard station near
Miami Beach, Florida, in September 1965.*

Your local radio and TV broadcasts will give you plenty of warning concerning an oncoming hurricane. Prepare yourself. Here are some precautions you can take:

- Store water in a clean bathtub and in jugs and bottles. Even if water still comes out of your faucets, it may not be safe for drinking.

- Board up large windows. Crisscross smaller ones with adhesive tape.

- Clean your yard. Bring everything loose indoors. Tools, flowerpots, boards, etc., become as dangerous as bullets when the wind shoots them along.

- Stay indoors. Don't go outside for any reason. The wind can knock you down. Flying objects or falling trees can hit you. Stay indoors away from the windows.

- Beware the eye of the storm. The wind may stop suddenly, and the skies may clear. But the hurricane is not past. You are in its eye and may remain there for half an hour or more. Then the wind will blow furiously again from the other direction.

Tornadoes come and go very quickly. However, if you are aware of the weather and looking in the right direction, you can often see them form.

Heavy clouds forming ragged lines across the sky indicate an approaching cold front, a mass of cold air. If the sky is very dark, it means that the clouds extend high into the sky. There is a good chance of a tornado forming if a dark cloud is accompanied by lots of thunder, lightning, hail, and rain. The bigger the hailstones, the more powerful the storm. But still, the cloud might not be a tornado. It might just be a heavy storm.

Now look at the bottom of the cloud. If it is forming a point sticking downward that is twisting around, you are watching the birth of a tornado.

If it is very dark outside or if the rain prevents you from seeing a twister form, you can tell one is being born by the sound. Tornadoes whistle like jumbo jetliners or huge factory whistles. The sound can be heard several miles away.

Here are some precautions you can take if you think a tornado is heading your way:

· Get indoors as fast as you can. Go to the nearest building.

· If you can't get indoors, lie flat in a ditch. Cover your head with your arms.

· If you are in a car or mobile home, get out and go to the nearest building.

· Once inside a building, go to the basement and get under a heavy table. Stay away from windows. Stay away from toasters, pipes, TV sets, etc. The lightning in the tornado kills more people than the tornado itself. It can come into your home along a wire or pipe.

· In schools and public buildings, move to the shelter or to the lowest level.

· RUN, DON'T WALK. A few seconds can mean the difference between life and death.

If you want to learn more about hurricanes and tornadoes, or if you would like to become a "storm spotter," write to NOAA, U.S. Department of Commerce, Rockville, Maryland 20852.

—63

Index